Cherokee Poetry

Kristine Marie Carrerow

Kristine Marie Carrerow
2020

First Printing: 2020

ISBN 978-0-578-23223-2

Kristine Marie Carrerow
San Jose, CA 95126

Dedication

For My Grandmother

Lora Lealer Ross

Author's Notes

This book was written to honor my grandmother, but also to inspire the generations that have been born after her. She was proud of her family and her childhood growing up in Cherokee Territory. She would be proud that her grandchildren, great-grandchildren, and great-great-grandchildren have become citizens of the Cherokee Nation.

The fact that as a young girl, her father, my great-grandfather, added her name to a census that would give her a number that would prove our birthright and grant his citizenship in the Cherokee Nation is phenomenal.

Lora Lealer Ross Donald would be incredibly excited and moved that her great-grandson, Doug, is now an accomplished artist as a Cherokee finger weaver as he weaves belts in patterns passed down for generations. Doug has also taken Cherokee language classes to learn a language that Lora spoke as a young girl.

To my children – Doug, Michelle, and Laki, and to my grandson, Tony – I will give to you the gift that my grandmother gave to me, the gift of a proud heritage.

We are Cherokee!

Table of Contents

Lora Lealer Ross. My Grandmother.

Lora Lealer Ross was born June 20, 1890 in Webbers Falls, Oklahoma, (Cherokee Territory). She was one of nine siblings. She was the next to the youngest child, and her lifelong mischief buddy would be her sister Nora, who was two years older. They grew up living on farmland in Cherokee Territory and as most little girls from that era, she learned to sew her clothes, did quilting and knitting, and she cooked and learned how to can her own food, which she did most of her life. She also spoke a second language, she was fluent in Cherokee.

Growing up, words were thrown out like "Oakies" or that we were Indian, but I did not know what an "Oakie" was, or what tribe of Indians. When I was old enough to drive, I would visit my grandmother, so I was about 16 years old when I was visiting and she exclaimed, "You know what Krissy? We're Cherokee!" She went on to tell me that my cousin Diana was researching our family tree and she found that we are direct descendants of Chief Oconastota. Her eyes were bright with excitement and I still did not exactly know how this would impact me, but I thought it was cool.

Years ago when people left Indian Territory they were looking for opportunities and most didn't look back. Being an American Native set you apart and not usually in a good way, so you just didn't mention it to people. I believe she loved her childhood and embraced the culture when she lived in Oklahoma. However, those days when she first came to California were for her to begin to live her life as a wife and mother, and so she did, bringing with her the skills she had learned as a young girl.

One time I visited my Grandmother, she was listening to a cassette tape with some very strange language on it. I asked her what it was and she said she was relearning Cherokee. "You're 85 years old. Why," I asked. "Because I want to and I won't live long enough to do all the things I want to do." She reclaimed who she was, although she would never deny that she was Cherokee, every document she filled out including my mother's birth certificate would proclaim her as 'white', but the Cherokee flame that smoldered in her soul could not be vanquished. In her 70's and 80's the Cherokee flame burned bright and by the time she passed away just shy of her 92nd birthday, that flame was lit in me. I still remember the most important word she said when proclaiming her birthright. She said that 'WE'RE Cherokee'. We certainly are.

Cherokee Fractions

When I first became a Citizen of the Cherokee

Nation, the first two questions people asked me were,

what percentage Cherokee are you and how much do

you get? Well, I have certain rights as a tribe member,

that were promised to my ancestors through treaties. As

far as my blood quantum, this is why I wrote the poem

'Cherokee Fractions.'

CHEROKEE FRACTIONS

"Just what percentage Cherokee?"
Is the question that you ask,
It seems that I must prove myself
You're taking me to task.

My ancestors did walk
A 'Trail of Tears' that took its toll,
My Great-Great Grandpa Andrew
Was a Cherokee Mounted Patrol.

My Grandmother was born
On an Oklahoma day,
The 'Dust Bowl' sent her packing
Out the California way.

Oconostota is my Grandfather
From six long 'greats' ago,
My Grandma made the 'Roll Call' list
That's something you should know.

So you see it's not percentage
But the person that is me,
So I'll tell you plain and simple
That I am a Cherokee!

Cherokee Landscape

At one time it seemed that all Indian tribes would be erased from the landscape of our nation. Like the, Phoenix, we did rise from the ashes. Tribes have once again established their people to be recognized as Sovereign Nations within the United States. We are no longer fading from the landscape of this nation.

CHEROKEE LANDSCAPE

In the landscape of a Nation
Once stood warriors so proud,
Strong women as their equals
Women wise and quite profound.

The men, they were the hunters
While the women farmed the land,
Then strangers came among them
Men who did not understand.

The strangers, they were different
They became a quiet fear,
Making natives to be strangers
Made them walked a 'Trail of Tears'.

Fading from the fabric
Of a Nation, not by choice,
They lost their lands to progress
Yet they did not lose their voice.

Just a number on a roster
Reservation refugees,
They had moved to other places
Yet remained still Cherokee.

Natives of the Nation
We no longer disappear,
We weave again the landscape
Strong in Spirit, we are here.

We're a growing population
We are proud and meant to be,
In the landscape of our Nation
You will see us, Cherokee!

Cherokee Trail

The sad story of our history of the tribal removal from our beloved lands must never be forgotten. The lives lost on the trail and the sadness of our people during that time must always be remembered and those people honored. Remember the removal.

CHEROKEE TRAIL

Broken, bruised, and blistered
Were the souls of those who came,
From the homes and farms of Georgia
Cherokee is their name.

Gathered and imprisoned
Forced to leave their lands,
Pushed onto a winter path
By government demand.

Sorrow overtook them
As they left their weak to die,
Forced ahead without them
Oh so haunted by their cries.

So the trail paved with bodies
And cemented with their tears,
Was not to be forgotten
We pay homage every year.

The ones who had survived them
Seized the spirit of their kin,
Moved to build again our Nation
Cherokee is strong again.

We strive to be community
Supporting young and old,
Cherishing our heritage
With stories to be told.

May our actions be in honor
For the ones we hold so dear,
For the Cherokees who lost their lives
Upon a 'Trail of Tears.'

Cherokee Solidarity

When the Standing Rock Sioux tried to stop the
Dakota Access Pipeline, other Native American Tribes
stood in solidarity with them. Our lands have been
taken and government treaties have been broken over
the years. We need to stand together and support each
other so that we do not lose any more of our lands or
rights.

CHEROKEE SOLIDARITY

I left my mark at Alcatraz
My heart at Wounded Knee,
I fight against the 'pipeline'
Yet they say it's destiny.

From Oahe Dam to Kinzua
The loss of land remains,
A trail of broken treaties
Fall to eminent domain.

You say to just get over it
It's been too many years,
Still the spirits haunt us
For the ones who shed their tears.

Buffy Sainte-Marie once said,
"It's in the past you say".
But if you chance to look around
It's happening today.

Poisoning our waters
Building through our lands,
Trying to divide us
When we try and take a stand.

We fight to keep our buffalo
Our water oil free,
We stand up for our people
For our tribe communities.

As our 'Nations' rise together
In our solidarity,
May we Natives band together
To affect our destiny.

Cherokee Missing

Because of the disconnect between tribal police, local police, and the federal government; many indigenous women are slipping through the cracks of law enforcement and the justice system. They are murdered, kidnapped and missing women and girls whose families cry out for justice and their cries have not been heard. We must break the silence and raise our voices for their sake as well as our own.

CHEROKEE MISSING

Indigenous, anonymous
More invisible each year,
Reservation women
Cloaked in silence, live in fear.

Who is missing, who is murdered
Who was raped in dark of night?
Were they taken and exploited
Or did they just take flight?

For some they lived in poverty
Or drugs became the norm,
The anger and the hopelessness
Became the perfect storm.

I will tell you, pay attention!
For these women's lives are dear,
Or you doom these tribal people
To another 'Trail of Tears'.

You drove these tribes to wastelands
Took their property supreme,
You made it that much harder
For them to weave their dreams.

So I beg you, not for silence
But to loudly lift a voice
And support these Native women
For there is no other choice.

For these women who go missing
We must finally realize,
That their value holds connection
To the value of our lives.

Cherokee Yanasi

Buffalo, or Bison, were at one time killed in great numbers. They were originally a life and survival source for many Native tribes. Associated with the Plains Indians, they were also in other areas of the United States as well. They were revered and respected as being connected to the tribe. Loss of habitat and irresponsible mass killing of these beautiful animals almost led to their extinction. They are being preserved in parks and on tribal land. In the Cherokee language, the word for Bison is Yanasi.

CHEROKEE YANASI

The brother who took care of us
Yanasi is his name,
He gave us food and clothes and tools
He roamed the woods and plains.

We were of kindred spirit
We did not waste their lives,
We used their meat for nourishment,
Their bones to make our knives.

We celebrate their spirit
We saw them as our friend,
It was not from our slaughter
That they faced a fateful end.

The bison faced their own 'Trail'
They were driven from their lands,
Or massacred in numbers
By ruthless, rifled hands.

Once more we see, Yanasi
On the Oklahoma plains,
They are here among the grasslands
As the population gains.

Cherokee Patriot

Ned Christie was a patriot to his people. He
advocated the communal living lifestyle they were
living and thought that by the government allotting
them parcels of land that the communities would suffer.
He was accused of murdering a lawman, but professed
his innocence. His people kept him hidden for 5 years,
but they eventually found and killed him. Later a
witness would come forth with the truth that he was
indeed innocent.

CHEROKEE PATRIOT

Ned Christie was a Patriot
A rascal now and then,
A champion for Cherokees
So strikes this writer's pen!

On Council to negotiate
For his community,
Solidify 'The Nation'
Keep our land as Cherokee.

One night he drank among his friends
His course would change that day,
A lawman had been murdered
It was blamed on Ned they say.

Well known for his Winchester
He had a deadly aim,
That fateful night, no rifle,
Did he carry, so Ned claims.

For five years he was sheltered
By his family and his friends,
Relentless were the marshals
So he met a bitter end.

When the dust had settled
Came a witness with the proof,
Ned Christie was an innocent
The witness held the truth.

So as this poet's pen declares
A Patriot Ned be,
A hero to his people
Proud to be a Cherokee!

Cherokee Sisters

This poem was inspired by my Grandmother's telling of a story about her and her sister, Nora (Aunt Nonie). When she spoke of her childhood, it was always with a fondness and laughter. She describes a farm, a horse, work mules and the fact that she was fluent in the Cherokee language. It wasn't always popular or safe to publicize your Native background, but when my cousin started searching our genealogy in the late 1960's, my Grandmother once again felt safe enough and very excited to let people know about her Cherokee heritage. After all, Chief Oconastota is her Great-Great-Great-Great Grandfather!

CHEROKEE SISTERS
(MY GRANDMOTHER'S STORY)

Two little girls of the Cherokee,
Running and playing so happy and free.
Lora and Nora apart by two years,
Descendents of those from the 'Trail of Tears'.

"A picnic", said Papa, "we'll have for today!
Our neighbor has melons, you girls know the way."
So they mounted on bareback, the old family mare.
Through a meadow and creek until they were there.

Their neighbor grew melons as big as a ball!
He handed one to them, "Be careful, don't fall."
Lora and Nora knew how to behave,
Said, "Wado." To their neighbor and cast him a
wave.

They got back to the creek for the mare to walk
through,
But this time surprise them is what she would do.
She leapt into the air and performed such a jump,
The girls, they held on but the melon went bump.

So they slid from the mare and the melon they ate.
They then started for home, they were so very late.
Papa took one look and he started to grin,
"Looks like you've had some adventure again"

They told him about the big jump and the fall.
How they ate a big melon as big as a ball.
How he certainly missed that incredible taste
But they couldn't just leave it, just leave it to
waste.
So the laughter ensued and it spread to all three.
Then erupted again when she told this to me.

Cherokee Culture

We do not live in the past, but we bring to the future our traditions from the past. We keep a living legacy by learning the Cherokee language, telling the stories of creation and relationships, playing the old music, yet composing new pieces. We are a living part of Cherokee culture. When we bead a necklace or finger-weave a belt, or make a ribbon shirt or tear dress, we are living what are ancestors created and creating anew what they taught us. By teaching the making of an arrow and teaching how to shoot that arrow, or teaching the making of a flute and teaching someone to play that flute, we carry on the creativity and passion of our ancestors. It is the heart of our people. So when we wear a necklace or a woven belt or greet each other with "Osiyo", we are just being who we are in the present…We are Cherokee.

CHEROKEE CULTURE

Our culture is alive
For the sake of our kin.
So no one can say,
"How it use to be, then."

Our language is living
It is spoken with skill,
We teach it and learn it
We're speaking it still.

Making a 'tear dress'
With fabric that's torn,
We weave with our fingers
The belts we adorn.

The art of an arrow
The workmanship grand,
The launch of that arrow
Through agile trained hands.

Not to live in the past
Yet to know where we're from
Teach the flute and tell stories
To pass on to our young.

For the tree that is rooted
Stands tall, strong, and free,
Our roots are tradition
We are Cherokee!

Cherokee Sovereignty

Sovereignty as a nation means that you are recognized as an independent nation by other nations and you govern yourself. The Cherokee Nation is recognized as a sovereign nation, and as such, we elect our Principal Chief and have been doing so since 1971. We currently have more than 370,000 tribal citizens. We have not disappeared, in fact, we still have our language, our arts, our music, and our stories…and of course our stories yet to be told.

CHEROKEE SOVEREIGNTY

We are a sovereign nation
We have our Native pride
We have our Chief, we have our laws
Cherokee is our tribe.

We pay homage to our ancestors
To those who came before,
Those who walked a 'Trail of Tears'
To those who wanted more.

Sometimes we have faltered
Sometimes we were down,
Every time we rose again
To claim our sacred ground.

So now we grow in numbers
Our Sovereignty intact,
For those who thought we disappeared
The Cherokee are back!

Made in the USA
Las Vegas, NV
17 January 2022

41633811R00021